Do Plants Have Babies?

Lisa J. Amstutz

rourkeeducationalmedia.com

ROURKE'S SCHOOL to HOME CONNECTIONS
BEFORE AND DURING READING ACTIVITIES

Before Reading: *Building Background Knowledge and Vocabulary*

Building background knowledge can help children process new information and build upon what they already know. Before reading a book, it is important to tap into what children already know about the topic. This will help them develop their vocabulary and increase their reading comprehension.

Questions and Activities to Build Background Knowledge:
1. Look at the front cover of the book and read the title. What do you think this book will be about?
2. What do you already know about this topic?
3. Take a book walk and skim the pages. Look at the table of contents, photographs, captions, and bold words. Did these text features give you any information or predictions about what you will read in this book?

Vocabulary: *Vocabulary Is Key to Reading Comprehension*
Use the following directions to prompt a conversation about each word.
- Read the vocabulary words.
- What comes to mind when you see each word?
- What do you think each word means?

Vocabulary Words:
- *pollen*
- *sprout*
- *stems*
- *stigma*

During Reading: *Reading for Meaning and Understanding*

To achieve deep comprehension of a book, children are encouraged to use close reading strategies. During reading, it is important to have children stop and make connections. These connections result in deeper analysis and understanding of a book.

 ### Close Reading a Text

During reading, have children stop and talk about the following:
- Any confusing parts
- Any unknown words
- Text to text, text to self, text to world connections
- The main idea in each chapter or heading

Encourage children to use context clues to determine the meaning of any unknown words. These strategies will help children learn to analyze the text more thoroughly as they read.

When you are finished reading this book, turn to the last page for an **After Reading Activity**.

Table of Contents

Baby Plants.................................... 4
From Flower to Seed 6
No Seeds Needed!.................... 16
Photo Glossary........................... 22
Activity... 23
Index.. 24
After Reading Activity 24
About the Author 24

Baby Plants

Do plants have babies?

Yes, they do! Plants spread in different ways.

From Flower to Seed

A flower makes dusty **pollen**.

It makes sweet nectar too.

Bzz! A bee sips the nectar.

Pollen sticks to its legs. It flies to a new flower.

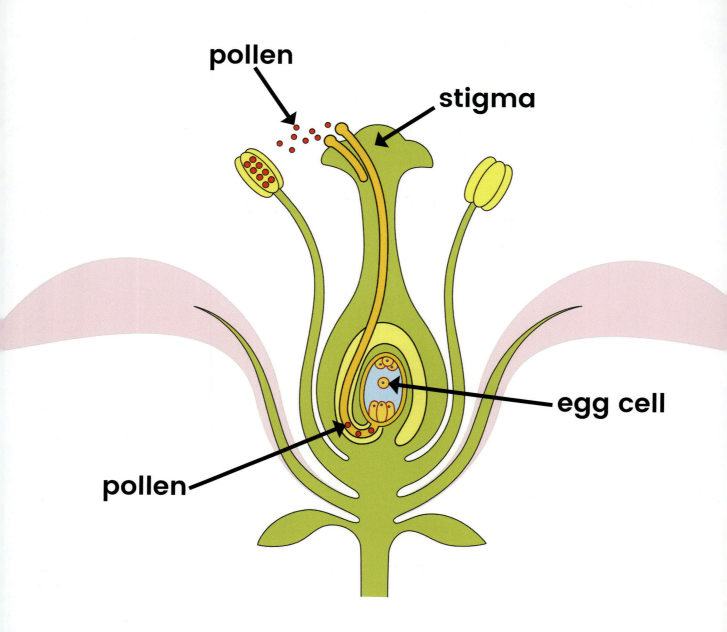

Pollen sticks to the flower's **stigma**. It meets an egg cell. It forms a seed.

Now the plant makes fruit. The seeds are inside.

The fruit falls to the ground. *Plop!*

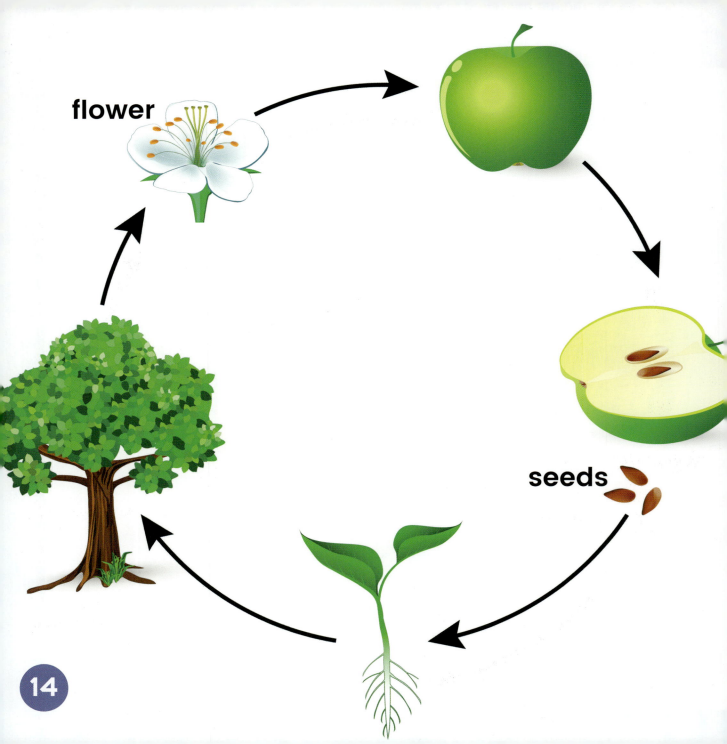

Seeds **sprout** and grow.

The new plants make flowers too.

No Seeds Needed!

Some plants can sprout without seeds. Some have long **stems** called *runners*.

The runner stretches from the parent plant. A new plant grows!

Buds can form on roots or stems.
New plants sprout and grow.

Look! Bulbs split into more bulbs.

Each grows a new plant.

Photo Glossary

pollen (PAH-luhn): Tiny grains produced in flowers. Pollen grains are the male cells of flowering plants.

sprout (sprout): To begin to grow and make shoots or buds.

stems (stemz): The tall parts of plants from which the leaves and flowers grow.

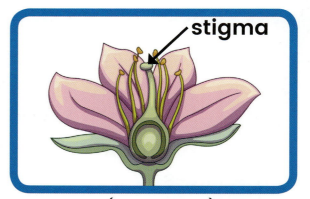

stigma (STIG-ma): The tip of the pistil of a flower, where pollen is received.

Activity

Planting Seeds

Seeds grow into new plants. Plant some bean seeds and watch them grow!

Supplies

four bean seeds   small glass jar
two paper towels   water in a spray bottle

Directions
1. Soak the seeds in water overnight.
2. Crumple two paper towels. Place them in the jar.
3. Spray the paper towels with water until they are damp, but not soaked.
4. Place the seeds between the paper towels and the sides of the jar so you can see them.
5. Set the jar in a sunny window. Keep the paper towels damp. Watch your seeds grow!

Index

bee 8
buds 18
flower(s) 6, 8, 11, 14, 15
fruit 12, 13
nectar 6, 8
seed(s) 6, 11, 12, 14, 15, 16

About the Author

Lisa J. Amstutz is the author of more than 100 children's books. She loves learning about science and sharing fun facts with kids. Lisa lives on a small farm with her family, two goats, a flock of chickens, and a dog named Daisy.

After Reading Activity

Look in your pantry or refrigerator. Can you find any seeds or fruits? What kinds of plants did they come from?

Library of Congress PCN Data

Do Plants Have Babies? / Lisa J. Amstutz
(My Life Science Library)
ISBN 978-1-73161-505-3 (hard cover)(alk. paper)
ISBN 978-1-73161-312-7 (soft cover)
ISBN 978-1-73161-610-4 (e-Book)
ISBN 978-1-73161-715-6 (e-Pub)
Library of Congress Control Number: 2019932048

Rourke Educational Media
Printed in the United States of America,
North Mankato, Minnesota

© 2020 Rourke Educational Media

All rights reserved. No part of this book may be reproduced or utilized in any form or by any means, electronic or mechanical including photocopying, recording, or by any information storage and retrieval system without permission in writing from the publisher.

www.rourkeeducationalmedia.com

Edited by: Kim Thompson
Produced by Blue Door Education for Rourke Educational Media.
Cover and interior design by: Nicola Stratford

Photo Credits: Cover logo: frog © Eric Phol, test tube © Sergey Lazarev, cover tab art © siridhata, cover photo © MISTER DIN, page background art © Zaie; page 4-5 © lovelyday12; page 7 © Marie C Fields; page 9 © Ikordela; page 10 © Aldona; page 12 © Aleksandra H. KossowskaGriskeviciene, page 13 © Lane V. Erickson; page 14 © Designua; page 16-17 © Volodymyr Nikitenko; page 19 © Vladimir Arndt; page 21 © Alexander Raths   All images from Shutterstock.com